EAST OF LOND

Pictures

Introd
Joyce

Since February 1987, my husband and I, along with Mr. B. J. Page, have produced and published a series of books called "Ilford Old and New". As the name suggests, this is of old pictures of Ilford, alongside present day views, illustrating the changes that have occured over the years.

Whilst collecting material for these books, we came across pictures of other areas, many of which were of the East of London. Some were of places frequented by our parents and grandparents and we could not resist taking a look to see what changes had taken place.

We were surprised by what we found, some places had changed beyond recognition, like the Mile End Road, while others, mostly churches and municipal buildings have remained the same.

We thought others might find the changes as fascinating as we did. Therefore, we would like to share with you, our first collection of old and new pictures of the East of London.

The pictures date from 1898 - 1988; to emphasise the changes that have occured over this period, the location of each present day scene is as close as possible to that of the earlier picture. With changes in road layouts and repositioning of buildings this was not always easy to achieve, this was especially true in the case of Angel Lane, but we feel we have managed to capture the changing scene.

Obviously the area to the East of London is vast and we could not cover it all in one book. Nevertheless we hope we have something for everyone, as we go from St. Katherine's Dock, bordering the City and the Thames, to Queen Elizabeth's Hunting Lodge which borders Epping Forest. We hope it will be of interest not only to local people but to those who have 'moved out' over the years.

ISBN 0 9512013 3 6
Ilford
May 1988 ©

St. Katherine's Dock, E1. About 1906 (Picture courtesy of Mr. Bill Austin). The original site was occupied by the Hospital of St. Katherine, founded in 1148 by Queen Matilda. In 1828 the site was developed by Thomas Telford with a series of basins and warehouses covering some 25 acres.

Below: The same view, 1988. Now used as a boat marina and the site of the World Trade Centre, etc.

The Jew's Market, Wentworth Street, E1. (Petticoat Lane) about 1898. (Picture B. J. Page collection). The name of Petticoat Lane probably originated from the many old clothes dealers who once traded in the area. Below: The same view, 1988.

Mile End Road, E1. About 1900 (Picture courtesy of Mr. Bill Austin). The above view, near Cambridge Heath Road, is looking east towards Bow.
Below: The same view 1988. Hidden from view by the notice board on the left, is the statue of William Booth, founder of the Salvation Army.

The People's Palace, Mile End Road, E1. About 1900 (Picture courtesy of Mr. Bill Austin). The building (now Queen Mary College) was designed by E. R. Robson and built in 1887. Originally the People's Palace was used to provide the East of London with an institution offering education as well as social activities. Below: A view of the old and new buildings of Queen Mary College, 1988. In 1984 the College celebrated the 50th anniversary of the granting of the Royal Charter by Queen Mary, when the college also took its present name.

Stepney Church (St. Dunstan's) Stepney High Street, E1. About 1906 (Picture B. J. Page collection). Rebuilt in the early 16th century on the site of two or three Saxon churches. Restored after the Second World War. Below: The same view, 1988.

West India Import Dock (now Canary Wharf) Isle of Dogs E14. About 1906 (Picture courtesy of Mr. Bill Austin). These were London's first enclosed wet docks and opened in 1802. The West India Docks covered some 243 acres.
Below: This view, taken in 1988, from Canary Wharf, shows part of the Docklands Light Railway. The Royal opening of the Railway took place on 30th July 1987 at Westferry Station.

Old Church East Ham.

East Ham Church, Norman Road, E6. About 1909 (Picture B. J. Page collection). The church (Saint Mary Magdalene) stands on an ancient site. There was a Roman cemetery close by, near what is now called Roman Road. The present church was built about 1130. The nine acre Churchyard became a Nature Reserve in 1976. In 1983 the Interpretative Centre was opened by H.M. The Queen. Both the Nature Reserve and the Centre are part of Passmore Edwards Museum. Below: A view of the church, 1988.

East Ham Town Hall, High Street South and junction of Barking Road E6. About 1945. (Picture B. J. Page collection). Built 1901 - 1903. Now Newham Town Hall. In 1965 East Ham and West Ham united as the London Borough of Newham under the Local Goverment Act, and incorporated North Woolwich and a small area of Barking west of the Roding.

Central Hall, Barking Road, East Ham, E6. About 1910. (Picture B. J. Page collection). This was the Methodist Central Hall which opened in 1906. The central hall, seating over 2,000 was built at a cost of £26,000. The building was demolished in 1969. Below: The same view, 1988.

High Street North, East Ham E6. About 1906. (Picture B. J. Page collection). The picture is looking towards Romford Road. The junction with Plashet Grove is on the left. Below: The same view, 1988.

11

Green Street, Upton Park E13. About 1905. (Reproduced by kind permission of the curator, Passmore Edwards Museum, Stratford E15). The picture is looking towards Romford Road. The junction with Harold Road is on the left. The boundary between East Ham and West Ham ran down the centre of the road. (Notice that Boots Chemist are still trading on the same site). There were once market stalls in Green Street (until the arrival of trams about 1904 when the traders moved to Queens Road). Below: The same view, 1988.

Balaam Street, Plaistow E13. Picture taken in July 1933. (Reproduced by kind permission of the curator, Passmore Edwards Museum, Stratford E15.) The view shows the east side of the road between numbers 48 and 56. On the corner is Plaistow Motors and Garage - notice that in the new picture below (1988) is a M.O.T. Testing Station on the same site. Balaam Street, first recorded between 1364 - 1365, took its name from the Balun family, who lived at Plaistow as early as 1183.

13

The Portway, West Ham. E15. About 1907. (Picture B. J. Page collection). The name Portway has been in use since at least the 16th century. The entrance to West Ham Park is shown on the left in the picture. For the last sixteen years of her life, Elizabeth Fry, the 19th century Quaker prison reformer lived at Upton Lane House (later "The Cedars") in the Portway. Below: The Portway, 1988.

West Ham Lane, Stratford E15. 1902. (Reproduced by kind permission of the curator, Passmore Edwards Museum, Stratford E15.) The picture shows the west side of the road between numbers 122 and 132. The buildings were demolished soon after 1902. Below: The same view, 1988. Number 128 is Newco Products (London Borough of Newham). The church shown is West Ham Tabernacle, built in 1903. The first church in West Ham Lane was erected in 1844 and in 1902 the building was sold to the council for road-widening and in part payment the council gave the present site.

Stratford Broadway, E15. About 1925. (Reproduced by kind permission of the curator, Passmore Edwards Museum, Stratford E15.) The obelisk in the centre of the picture was erected in 1861 to the memory of Samuel Gurney, Quaker banker and philanthropist. (Brother of Elizabeth Fry). Gurney was the owner of West Ham Park. He worked for penal reform and the abolition of slavery.
Below: The same view, 1988.

The Grove, Stratford, E15. About 1904. (Picture B. J. Page collection). The picture shows St. John's Church which was built in 1834 and designed by Edward Blore in the early English Style. During the Second World War the church was badly damaged by bombing and was restored in 1951. The Grove is named after a mansion which once stood in the area. Below: The same view, 1988.

Town Hall, Stratford, E15. About 1906. (Picture B. J. Page collection). The Town Hall was opened in 1869 and enlarged in 1885. In July 1986, the building was re-opened by H.M. The Queen, after complete restoration following a serious fire. The former Fire Brigade Station, adjoining the Town Hall, was built in 1869. (In 1964 a new station was opened in Romford Road).

West Ham Church, Church Street North, E15. About 1906. (Picture B. J. Page collection). The church (All Saints) dates from the 12th century and was altered in the 13th century. Its long history includes many additions and restoring. From the 16th century onwards All Saints church remained the only Anglican place of worship until the building of St. Mary Plaistow (1830) and St. John Stratford (1834). Below: The same view, 1988.

Angel Lane, Stratford, E15. About 1954. (Picture courtesy of Cranley Commercial Calendars Ltd.) Market Stalls in Angel Lane started to decline about 1969 when the Angel Lane area was awaiting redevelopment. Below: Stratford Centre, 1988, which occupies the former Angel Lane Market area.

Entrance to Great Eastern Railway Works, Stratford, E15. Early 1900's. (Picture B. J. Page collection). The works at Stratford were established by the Northern and Eastern Railway in 1839-1840. In 1848 they were taken over by the Eastern Counties Railway and became the headquarters of the Great Eastern Railway in 1862. The original site was between the line running to Temple Mills and Angel Lane. The above view shows the entrance into Angel Lane, opposite the Railway Public House. Below: The same view, 1988.

Woodgrange Road, Forest Gate, E7. (Junction of Romford Road). About 1903. (Picture B. J. Page collection). In the distance can be seen the first Forest Gate Methodist Church, built 1881-1882. A new church was opened in 1962. Archibald Cameron Corbett was the principal developer of the Woodgrange Estate. When the development was completed in 1892 it consisted of 1,160 houses.

The double fronted houses cost about £530 leasehold and smaller terraced homes cost about £330. The Princess Alice Public House can be seen on the left in both pictures. Below: The same view, 1988.

Earlham Grove, Forest Gate, E7. About 1906. (Picture B. J. Page collection). Earlham Hall on the right was built in 1897 and became the headquarters of the Metropolitan Academy of Music. The building is now used as a place of worship by the Holy Order of Cherubim and Seraphim Church. Below: The same view, 1988.

High Road, Leytonstone, E11. About 1954. (Picture courtesy of Cranley Commercial Calendars Ltd.) The picture shows part of St. John's Church. The present building was opened in 1833. Also shown is part of the Rialto Cinema, which opened in 1911 as the Rink Picture Palace, (converted from Leytonstone Roller Skating Rink). It became the Rialto in 1927, the Granada in 1967 and closed in 1974. Adjoining the Rialto was Bearman's Ltd, drapers and house furnishers. The site of the cinema and Bearman's Stores is now occupied by the Co-Op Leo's Supermarket, as shown in the photograph below (1988).

24

The Green Man, Leytonstone, E11. About 1912. (Picture courtesy of Mr. C. Clerkin). The picture shows The Green Man Public House (the present building stands further back). A Green Man Inn is recorded as early as 1668. Leytonstone High Road, as a link in the London Epping route, was by 1594 more important than Leyton High Road. The tram in the picture had started its journey from Aldgate. Below: The same view, 1988.

25

High Street, Wanstead, E11. About 1900. (Picture B. J. Page collection). This view, looking towards The George corner, shows the shop of W. H. Clayden, Grocer. The site of the original shop is now Websters Butchers. The cottage on the corner of the High Street and Woodbine Place was also known as "Claydens Corner" and the site is now occupied by Land and Company, Estate Agents. For many years Edwin Fisher, house furnishers, also had a shop there. Below: The same view, 1988.

Station Parade, Snaresbrook, E11. Pictured in the early 1940's. (Picture B. J. Page collection). The station was opened in 1856 and was then part of the Eastern Counties Railway. Below: The same view, 1988.

Walthamstow. Church End.

Church End, Walthamstow E17. About 1912. (Picture B. J. Page collection). This picture shows the Almshouses which were founded in 1795 by Mrs. Mary Squires. The inscription above the almshouses reads: "These houses are erected and endowed forever by Mrs. Mary Squires, widow, for the use of six decayed tradesmen's widows of this parish and no other Ano Domi 1795". Below: A view of The Squire's Almshouses, 1988. In the background is the tower of St. Mary's Church. The building dates back to the 12th Century. Nearby is Vestry House, originally the parish workhouse, now the Waltham Forest Museum of Local History.

High Street, Walthamstow, E17. About 1954. (Picture courtesy of Cranley Commercial Calendars Ltd). On the right can be seen the former Walthamstow Palace Music Hall, opened in 1903 and demolished in 1960. Opposite, on the left, was the Carlton Cinema which opened in 1913. The cinema closed in 1964.
Below: The same view 1988.

Station Road, Chingford, E4. About 1910. (Picture B. J. Page collection). Station Road was previously known as Maddox Lane, which was recorded in 1790. It may also have been called the High Street, being regarded as a continuation of what is now The Ridgeway. The present name came into use after the building of the new Chingford Station in 1878, but Maddox Lane remained, intermittently, in official use until 1904 for that part of the road between the station and Bury Path. Below: The same view, 1988.

Queen Elizabeth's Hunting Lodge, Chingford, E4. About 1906. (Picture courtesy of Mr. Bill Austin). The building, which dates back to the 16th century, served as a grandstand from which the Queen and her guests could watch the hunt. To the left of the picture is part of the former stables and coaching house of the Royal Forest Hotel. Below: The same view, 1988. The building is now used as the Epping Forest Museum.

31

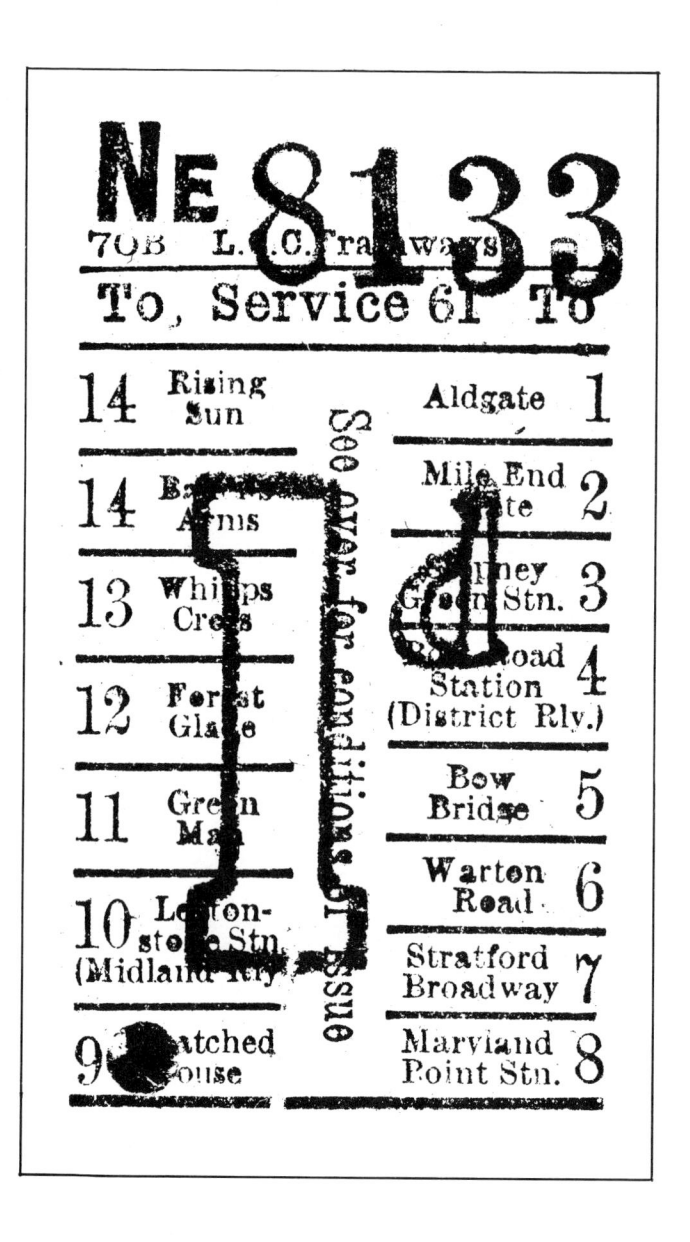

London County Council Tram Ticket (1930's) issued for Tram number 61 Aldgate to the Rising Sun, Walthamstow.